Cal
Ripken
Jr.

Cal Ripken Jr.

Oriole Ironman

Stew Thornley

Lerner Publications Company ■ Minneapolis

*To Howard and Phyllis Thornley, who raised me properly —
as a baseball fan*

ACKNOWLEDGMENTS

The photographs in this book are reproduced through the courtesy of:
© Jerry Wachter Photography Ltd., pp. 1, 2, 6, 8, 11, 26, 31, 32, 35, 36,
43, 44, 48, 53; National Baseball Library, Cooperstown, N.Y., pp. 11, 60;
Violet Ripken, pp. 12, 14, 16, 19, 20, 23; UPI/Bettmann, pp. 29, 38, 40,
54; Minneapolis Star Tribune, p. 50; Al Kermisch, p. 61; Mary Anne
Page, *Southeast*, p. 64; Front and back cover photos: © Jerry Wachter
Photography Ltd.

This book is available in two editions:
Library binding by Lerner Publications Company
Soft cover by First Avenue Editions
241 First Avenue North
Minneapolis, Minnesota 55401

LIBRARY OF CONGRESS CATALOGING-IN-PUBLICATION DATA

Thornley, Stew.
  Cal Ripken, Jr. : Oriole ironman / Stew Thornley.
     p.   cm
  Summary: A biography of the Baltimore Orioles team member known for his play as shortstop.
     ISBN 0-8225-0547-9 (lib. bdg.)
     ISBN 0-8225-9624-5 (pbk.)
     1. Ripken, Cal, 1960-   —Juvenile Literature. 2. Baseball
players—United States—Biography—Juvenile literature.
3. Shortstop (Baseball)—Juvenile literature. [1. Ripken, Cal,
1960-   . 2. Baseball players.] I. Title.
GV865.R47T48   1992
796.357'092—dc20
[B]   92-5000
                                                                      CIP
                                                                       AC

Manufactured in the United States of America

International Standard Book Number: 0-8225-0547-9 (lib. bdg.)
International Standard Book Number: 0-8225-9624-5 (pbk.)
Library of Congress Catalog Card Number: 92-5000

1   2   3   4   5   96   95   94   93   92

Contents

1

A New Beginning

It is the first Saturday of the 1991 baseball season in Arlington, Texas. The Baltimore Orioles prepare to face the Texas Rangers. The afternoon's rain has ended, but the ballpark is still damp, and the evening chilly.

So far this season, the bat of Oriole shortstop Cal Ripken, Jr., has been as cold as the weather. In Baltimore's first three games of the season, Cal has mustered only a pair of singles.

Cal has often had early-season slumps, but can he rebound this time? Can his batting average rise along with the springtime temperature as it did in earlier years? Is Cal—a 10-year veteran—simply wearing out?

Cal took forever getting started last season. As late as mid-June of 1990, his batting average was still very low—just over .200. Only a summer surge saved his season, raising his average to .250 and his power numbers to 21 home runs and 84 runs batted in. Those are statistics most players—especially shortstops, who are usually valued for their defense more than for their batting—would envy. But the Orioles and the Baltimore fans expect a lot from Cal. Besides having the virtues that make a shortstop shine—sure hands, great range, an accurate throwing arm—Cal is supposed to light up the scoreboard. He is Baltimore's ironman, the guy who should do it all.

Perhaps he had done too much too early. His first two full years in the majors were pure magic. In 1982 he was voted the American League's Rookie of the Year. The next season, he was the league's Most Valuable Player and helped lead the Orioles to a World Series championship. Cal had achieved a degree of excellence that would be hard for any player—including himself—to match.

When he was unable to do so, his critics started speaking up. By 1990, despite his summertime rebound at the plate, the criticism had become loud and constant.

At the heart of the criticism was The Streak—Cal's string of consecutive games played. Since May 30, 1982, Cal had started every one of the Orioles' games.

By mid-June of 1990, Cal had played more consecutive games than anyone in baseball history except Lou Gehrig, the New York Yankees' legendary first baseman. Gehrig's string of 2,130 games—which spanned nearly 14 seasons from 1925 to 1939—had earned him the nickname "Iron Horse."

Cal's streak, however, had some people saying that he should take a day off occasionally—that his lack of rest was hurting his hitting. "Ripken's pursuit [of Gehrig's record] is counterproductive both to himself and his team," said Steve Hirdt of the Elias Sports Bureau early in the 1990 season.

The fans were even harder on Cal. On June 12 of 1990—when Cal eclipsed Everett Scott's mark of 1,307 consecutive games and logged the second-longest playing streak in history—the fans at Baltimore's Memorial Stadium booed.

Through it all, Cal maintained that his hitting woes were unrelated to the streak. He knew, however, that the best way to stop the negative talk was to regain his batting stroke. A quick start in 1991 would be a big step in that direction.

So, on a damp evening in Arlington, Texas, Cal steps into the batter's box with something to prove. It's the first inning of this game against the Rangers. Cal's teammate Randy Milligan is on first base. Texas lefthander Kenny Rogers delivers, and Cal lines the pitch toward center. The center fielder slips on the

Yankee legend Lou Gehrig holds the record for consecutive games played—2,130.

rain-soaked turf. The ball sails over his head and rolls to the base of the fence. Milligan scores, and Cal pulls into third with a triple.

The bases are loaded when Cal comes up for the second time. He laces a fastball up the middle for a single to score two more runs.

In the fourth inning, he hits a ball that is caught by the Rangers' left fielder on the warning track. In the sixth inning, though, he doesn't give the outfielders a chance, as he puts one over the fence for a two-run homer. Then, in the eighth, he drills another two-run homer, this one to straightaway center.

Cal finishes the night with four hits, two home runs, and seven runs batted in, just two short of the team record.

Cal is on his way.

The Ripken kids: Cal Jr. (in back) and (left to right) Ellen, Bill, and Fred

2
Starting Out

A lot of kids grow up playing catch with Dad—nothing unusual about that. For Cal Ripken, Jr., though, these games of catch usually took place on a professional baseball diamond, not in the backyard or a vacant lot.

Cal's father, Calvin Edward Ripken, Sr., had been with the Baltimore Oriole organization since before Cal Jr. was born. From 1956 to 1974, Cal Sr. worked with several of the Orioles' minor-league farm teams—sometimes as a player, sometimes as a manager, sometimes as both.

On August 24, 1960, Cal Jr. was born in Havre de Grace, Maryland. At the time his dad was in Topeka, Kansas, nearly half a continent away.

Cal in 1962 (top). Cal started his baseball career early, here with his sister, Ellen (right).

14

Cal Sr. was a catcher for Fox Cities (Wisconsin), an Oriole farm club in the Three-I League, and celebrated the birth of his first son by driving in the winning run in the 10th inning against Topeka.

Cal Jr. inherited athletic talent from both his dad and his mom. Vi Ripken first attracted her future husband's attention while she was playing softball in high school. "She was a pretty good hitter herself," says Cal Sr. He could later say the same of his daughter, Ellen, who was born the year before Cal.

The other members of the Ripken clan have also demonstrated abilities with a bat and glove, but Fred, a year younger than Cal Jr., never got baseball fever. According to Cal Jr., Fred is "a natural athlete, maybe the best of all of us. But he never wanted to play that much. He wanted to do other things in life. I think he just got tired of baseball." The Ripkens' other son, Bill—four years younger than Cal—is a totally different story. He has followed his father's and brother's footsteps all the way to the diamond at Baltimore's Memorial Stadium.

Although baseball was in their blood, Cal Sr. and Vi were careful not to force the game on any of their children. Even so, Cal Jr. could not get enough of the sport. "From the time he was a little tyke," said Vi, "all Cal ever wanted to be was a ballplayer."

Having a father who was a baseball player was not necessarily an advantage for the young Ripkens.

Cal Sr. once managed the Tri-Cities (Washington) Atoms baseball team. On Father's Day in 1965, Cal (kneeling) was joined by all four of his children.

Traveling for the Oriole organization kept Cal Sr. away from his family for much of the year.

Every spring, Vi and the children would remain at home in Aberdeen, Maryland, while Cal Sr. took off to join whichever team he was playing for that year. The stops in his playing career included Phoenix, Arizona; Wilson, North Carolina; Amarillo, Texas; and Little Rock, Arkansas.

In 1961 he began managing some of the Oriole farm clubs and had to make temporary homes for himself in several parts of the United States while his family stayed in Maryland. By 1975, the year he settled down with the parent club in Baltimore, Cal Sr. had played for or managed teams in 15 cities.

As a result, Cal Sr. had few chances to watch his sons play in Little League. Cal's mother was the one who cheered from the bleachers and who taught Cal—and later Bill—how to hit. "When I look back on it," says Cal, "I really have to tip my hat to my mom. She took me to all of my games, congratulated me if I did well, consoled me if I didn't."

But even though his father wasn't always around, Cal Jr. said theirs was a close family. After school let out for the summer, the Ripkens were together again. Vi would load the family into the car and take off to wherever Dad was that year.

Having a father in baseball did offer some great benefits. The Ripken kids had the chance to hang around a ballpark and learn from players good enough to earn a living at the game.

During the three summers that his dad managed a team in Asheville, North Carolina—from 1972 to 1974—Cal Jr. was at the park every day. "I'd watch those games intently. Other kids would be wandering through the stands, but I'd be sitting behind the screen finding out what the pitchers were throwing. After the game, I'd start asking my dad questions. I always wanted to know why he did something.

"By the time I was ready to play, I knew the proper way to do things. I knew the Oriole way."

As the days grew shorter—and the baseball season entered its last few weeks—Cal returned home to start another year of school. He was a good student, especially in math, at Aberdeen High School.

By the time Cal Jr. was in high school, his dad was working his way up to the major leagues. In 1975 Cal Sr. worked as a scout for the Orioles, helping them find and evaluate young players. He still traveled a great deal, but at least he was stationed at home in Maryland.

The next year, the elder Ripken was back in uniform, as a coach for the Orioles. This gave Cal Jr. the chance to talk baseball with some of the team's stars and learn from them.

"I had the luxury of taking ground balls with Mark Belanger," said Cal, speaking of the Orioles' outstanding shortstop, whose place Cal would eventually take in the Baltimore infield.

At Aberdeen High, Cal earned a school letter as a member of the soccer team. But it was on a baseball diamond, not a soccer pitch, that he stood out.

He played shortstop—putting to use the lessons he had learned from Belanger—and also pitched. The strong right arm that allowed him to throw runners out from deep in the hole also enabled him to star on the mound.

Cal Jr. (wearing a cap), Fred, and Vi watch Cal Sr.'s team, the Aberdeen (South Dakota) Pheasants in 1964.

Cal played for Aberdeen High School as a freshman. By his senior year (opposite), he had gained seven inches and 50 pounds.

In 1978, his senior year, Cal pitched 60 innings and struck out 100 batters while allowing only six earned runs. He also batted .492 and drove in 29 runs in 20 games. Cal was the winning pitcher in the Maryland High School Class A championship game, hurling a two-hitter and striking out 17.

When he started high school, he stood only 5 feet, 7 inches tall and weighed just 128 pounds. By the time he graduated, he had grown to 6 feet, 2 inches and added more than 50 pounds to his frame.

Scouts from many different major-league teams came to see Cal play at Aberdeen High. He also attracted the attention of several colleges who wanted him to play for them. The U.S. Military Academy at West Point even wanted him to play soccer there. Cal could easily have gone to college—his grades were more than good enough—but he was eager to play professional baseball. Knowing that so many teams had been scouting him, Cal wanted to see which of them would draft him.

In the end it was the team he had grown up rooting for and the organization his father had long worked for—the Baltimore Orioles. Since he had been drafted so highly—in the third round—Cal gave no more thought to college.

Even though he called the Orioles "my only team—for obvious reasons," part of him hoped that some other team would take him. "I didn't want to think that I was only being drafted because of my dad," he explained. "But what it finally boiled down to was that I wanted to be an Oriole."

He quickly signed his first pro contract and reported to the Orioles' minor-league team at Bluefield, West Virginia, in the Appalachian League. He played mostly shortstop that season, but by the following year he had moved over a position and was spending more time at third base.

He was still growing—he finally topped out at 6 feet, 4 inches—and his size was considered a drawback for a shortstop. Traditionally, shortstops have been slight and fast. The nicknames of some of the game's greatest shortstops—men such as "Rabbit" Maranville, "Pee Wee" Reese, and Phil Rizzuto, known affectionately as "Scooter"—paint an image of the small, swift shortstop.

The Orioles thought that, in the long run, third base would be Cal's best position. He started playing that position regularly for Oriole farm clubs in 1979, initially with Miami in the Florida State League and then with Charlotte in the Southern League.

During his first two seasons in the minors, Cal was less than great at the plate—only eight home runs. In 1980, however, he broke loose with 25 homers.

Cal (front row, second from right) was the captain of the Aberdeen team. He played shortstop and pitched.

By 1981 Cal had progressed to the Orioles' top minor-league team, the Rochester (New York) Red Wings in the International League. Early in the season, he played in a historic game between the Red Wings and the Pawtucket (Rhode Island) Red Sox. Rochester carried a 1-0 lead into the last of the ninth, but Pawtucket scored to send the game into extra innings—lots of them.

The Red Wings again appeared on the verge of winning when they scored in the 21st inning, but the Red Sox retied the game with a run in the bottom of the frame. From there, it was all goose eggs until Pawtucket finally pushed a run across in the last of the 33rd, ending the longest game ever played in organized baseball. Cal had two hits in 13 at bats and played every inning of the marathon contest. His ironman performance was a sign of things to come.

Cal hit .288 with 23 home runs and was named the International League's Rookie of the Year in 1981, even though he was no longer around at the end of the season. On August 8th, he had been called up to the Baltimore Orioles.

3

A Hard Act to Follow

The Orioles had planned to leave Cal at Rochester for the entire season, but some unusual events brought him an early invitation to the parent club.

In June of 1981, major-league players went on strike. The labor-management dispute caused a 50-day interruption in the season, wiping out the middle third of the year. When the strike ended, the owners decided to start over with a "new" season. They declared that the teams leading each division at the time of the strike were the champions of the first half. These teams would then play off against the champions of the second half of the season for the right to advance to the league championship series.

Cal's former tutor, Mark Belanger (in background), was the Orioles'
regular shortstop in 1981. So when he joined the team, Cal often
played third base.

The Orioles had finished the pre-strike season in second place in the American League Eastern Division, two games behind the New York Yankees. They had 51 games scheduled in the second half of the season and would have to finish first in the division if they were to advance in the playoffs.

Hank Peters, the Orioles' general manager, explained the decision to add Cal to the roster. "With only 51 games, we have to have the strongest team possible. We feel that Ripken makes us the strongest team."

The promotion to Baltimore reunited Cal with his dad, who coached third base for the Orioles. The two even shared rides to and from Memorial Stadium.

Cal didn't have to wait long to get his first taste of the majors. The Orioles' second-half opener, against the Kansas City Royals, went extra innings. In the bottom of the 12th, Cal entered the game as a pinch runner for Ken Singleton, who had doubled. One batter later, John Lowenstein singled, and Cal raced home from second with the winning run.

Cal saw action at two positions. He filled in at shortstop for his former tutor, Mark Belanger, and also provided third baseman Doug DeCinces with an occasional rest. Mostly, though, he sat on the bench and watched. Of the team's last 20 games, Cal appeared in only 2, both times as a pinch runner. He finished his brief season in the majors with just five hits for a .128 batting average.

The Orioles were good that strike-interrupted season, but they came up short. They did not win a division title in the second half of the season, so there was no playoff spot for Baltimore, at least not that year.

Cal had played in so few games with the Orioles in 1981 that he was still considered a rookie in 1982. And by the spring of that year, he was ready for full-time duty.

During the off-season, DeCinces had been traded to the California Angels for outfielder Danny Ford. Belanger was also gone, having signed as a free agent with the Los Angeles Dodgers. Both positions on the left side of the infield were open, but again the Orioles decided that Cal was best suited for third base.

Cal's manager his first full year in the majors was a longtime Oriole—Earl Weaver. Weaver had been at the Orioles' helm since 1968 and had guided them to four American League pennants and one world championship. Like Cal Sr., Weaver had managed some of the Orioles' minor-league teams in earlier years. In fact, Weaver had been the elder Ripken's manager at Fox Cities in 1960.

Before the opening of the 1982 season, Weaver had announced that this would be his last year as Baltimore's manager. The players hoped to provide their skipper with one last appearance in a World Series before he retired.

They got off to a good start with a 13-5 win over Kansas City in the opener. His first time up, Cal provided the Orioles with an early boost when he connected for a two-run homer off the Royals' Dennis Leonard. He added a double and a single later in the game.

Reporters found Cal cleaning leaves from the gutter of his townhouse the day he was named Rookie of the Year.

But Cal got only four hits in his next 55 at bats, and by May his average had dropped to .117.

Cal's slump mirrored some tough times for the whole team. The Orioles suffered a nine-game losing streak in May that left them in last place. Weaver felt pressure to pull Ripken from the lineup.

The veteran manager, however, stuck with his rookie. "It's too early to start making changes," he said. "The thing is, the kid never really looks bad up there at the plate. He's not being outclassed and he's not getting overpowered."

Late May brought a turnaround, and Cal began a hot streak. Cal and the Orioles began their rise together. While Baltimore climbed in the standings, Cal's name moved up the list of American League hitters.

On May 29th, Cal sat out the second game of a doubleheader against Toronto. That game would earn a place in history as Cal's last game on the bench for a long, long time. The next day, he was back in the lineup—the start of his incredible streak of consecutive games played.

A few days later in Minnesota, he started the game but was removed for a pinch hitter in the ninth inning. This would be the last time for nearly five-and-a-half years he would even be taken out of a game.

Even though Cal suffered a slump at bat, his play in the field was steady. He went 44 games at third base without an error. But his stay at third was brief.

Cal and Eddie Murray were good friends and a powerful tandem in the Oriole batting order.

On July 1st, he was back at the position he had often played in high school—shortstop.

Weaver cited Cal's hitting as the reason for the switch. "It's always been easier to find a third baseman who can hit the ball out of the park than a shortstop. You never know, Rip might be a great shortstop. He's played the position before."

Weaver showed additional confidence in Cal by moving him up in the batting order. Cal would often benefit from having first baseman Eddie Murray hitting behind him. With the always-dangerous Murray waiting on deck, pitchers would be reluctant to "pitch around" Cal. No pitcher wanted to walk Cal and have a runner on base when Murray stepped to the plate. This would mean more good pitches for Cal to hit.

Cal snags one on the run.

The change in the batting order worked. Ripken and Murray gave the Orioles a tremendous one-two punch that terrorized opposing pitchers. Meanwhile, the Orioles continued their pursuit of first place.

On the final weekend of the season, the Milwaukee Brewers came to Baltimore for a four-game series. The first-place Brewers held a three-game lead over Baltimore, but it disappeared when the Orioles swept a doubleheader on Friday night and then won again on Saturday.

The entire season came down to one game, which went to the Brewers. Robin Yount had four hits, including two home runs, to lead Milwaukee to a 10-2 win and the American League East crown.

Yount was voted the American League's Most Valuable Player for 1982, outpolling Cal's teammate Murray, who had also logged a very strong season.

The Orioles had not been able to bounce back completely from their slow start, but Cal had definitely bounced back from his. He ended the year with 28 home runs and 93 runs batted in, a performance good enough to make him American League Rookie of the Year.

When training camp started the next season, Earl Weaver, who had shown so much faith in Cal, was gone. Cal would play for a different manager in 1983—Joe Altobelli, another longtime manager in the Orioles' farm system.

Under their new manager, the Orioles avoided the early-season slump that had plagued them in 1982. They quickly rose to first place, a spot they held for 115 of the season's 181 days. During the entire 1983 season, the Orioles never trailed a division leader by more than three games—and Baltimore never trailed anyone at all from August 26 to the end of the season.

Despite injuries that kept two of the top Oriole pitchers—Mike Flanagan and Jim Palmer—out for extended periods, the Baltimore pitching staff posted the American League's second-best earned-run average. It was that kind of season—dedicated play from an entire squad eager to extend its season into October.

The Orioles were awesome on offense. The Ripken-Murray power tandem was backed up by Ken Singleton, Gary Roenicke, John Lowenstein, and Dan Ford, and the Orioles led the American League in home runs. With Al Bumbry and John Shelby adding speed on the bases, the Orioles averaged nearly five runs per game, second-best in the league.

The Oriole machine sputtered briefly in August. A seven-game losing streak dropped them to fourth place. But on August 13, Cal helped put the brakes on the Orioles' skid. Cutting loose with his smooth, powerful swing, he delivered a two-run homer in the eighth inning to break a 2-2 tie with the White Sox. The Orioles won that game, as well as 33 of their next 43. They clinched their division in September.

Cal is one of the most feared hitters in the majors.

Cal played in the 1983 World Series against the Philadelphia Phillies.

Down the stretch, Ripken and Murray were phenomenal. Eddie hit nine home runs, scored 32 runs, and drove in another 32 in his last 37 games. Cal, in his final 44 games, hit .394 with 10 home runs, 30 RBI, and 42 runs scored. In one game at Minnesota in early September, Cal had five hits, including two home runs and two doubles, to set a team record of 13 total bases.

Many of the Orioles, including Murray, Singleton, Flanagan, and Palmer, had been through the playoffs before—when the Orioles had lost to the Pittsburgh Pirates in the 1979 World Series.

Their mere presence in that 1979 series gave Baltimore a core of players with postseason experience. These veterans could take some pressure off the newcomers like Cal as they prepared to face the Chicago White Sox in the American League Championship Series.

Chicago won the opener, but the Orioles roared back to win the pennant and the chance to play the Philadelphia Phillies in the World Series.

Once again Baltimore lost the first game and then won three in a row. The Orioles led, three games to one, against the Phillies when the fifth game of the best-of-seven series got underway in Philadelphia. In the finale, Scott McGregor pitched a shutout, and Eddie Murray hit two home runs. The last out in the 5-0 victory came when Garry Maddox hit a line drive to Ripken. After catching the liner, Cal gleefully slammed the ball to the ground—a fitting start to the Orioles' celebration of their World Series championship.

For Cal, it had not been an outstanding series; he had hit only .167. The season as a whole, however, had been spectacular: a .318 batting average, 27 home runs, 102 RBI; in addition, he led the league with 121 runs, 211 hits, and 47 doubles.

The writers who vote for the league's Most Valuable Player had a tough choice to make, because Eddie Murray, with 33 home runs and 111 RBI, also merited strong consideration.

In 1983 Cal (right) was the American League's Most Valuable Player, and Dale Murphy was MVP of the National League.

When the ballots were in, though, Cal had edged out his friend and teammate and was named the American League's Most Valuable Player. He was also named the major leagues' Player of the Year by the *Sporting News.*

It was quite a beginning for the young shortstop: Rookie of the Year his first season, and Most Valuable Player and a World Series championship his second.

What could he possibly do for an encore?

During spring training in 1985, manager Joe Altobelli gives instructions to his second-base combination—Cal Ripken, Jr., and Rich Dauer.

4

A Family Affair

Despite so much glory so early, Cal continued working hard. He hung tough as the American League's premier shortstop in the following years and was an annual starter in the All-Star Game. The Orioles, however, had fallen upon hard times.

With the team mired in fourth place in mid-June of 1985, Altobelli was fired as manager. Earl Weaver came out of retirement to replace him, but the change in managers had little effect on the team. The following season, in 1986, the Orioles lost 42 of their last 56 games and finished last for the first time since moving to Baltimore in 1954. A frustrated Weaver stepped down again, this time for good.

The Orioles didn't have to look far for a manager. The day after the 1986 season ended, they announced that their longtime coach and former minor-league manager—Cal Ripken, Sr.—would be the new skipper.

Cal Sr. had been passed over twice for the managing job—first when Altobelli got the job in 1983 and then when Weaver replaced Altobelli two-and-a-half years later.

"Rip is not getting this job just because he has been a loyal employee for a long time," said general manager Hank Peters. "Cal is getting the job because we think he's the one who can turn this team around and get it heading back in the right direction."

The Orioles pointed out that Cal Jr.'s role on the team also had nothing to do with their hiring Cal Sr. The elder Ripken was equally quick to point out that he would show no favoritism to Cal Jr.

Cal Sr. showed what he meant in September of 1987—he took his son out of a game, the first time Cal Jr. had been pulled since June 4, 1982. Cal's consecutive-game streak would continue, but his string of consecutive innings—8,243—had come to an end, courtesy of his father.

Cal Jr. didn't question the decision. "It was a surprise [to be taken out]," he said, "but I didn't feel I needed an explanation. The manager's job is to make the moves. It just so happens, in this case, that the manager is my father."

Cal gets a handshake and a pat from his father as he rounds the bases after a home run in 1989.

Father-son combinations on the same team have been rare in the majors, but the Ripkens were not the first. Connie Mack had managed his son Earle on the Philadelphia Athletics more than 60 years earlier; Yogi Berra did the same with his son Dale on the New York Yankees in 1984 and 1985; and Jim Hegan was a coach for the Yankees when his son Mike played for them in the 1960s. After the Ripkens, two more father-son pairs have been on the same team. In 1991 Hal McRae was named manager of the Kansas City Royals, for whom his son Brian played. The year before that, Ken Griffey, Sr., and Ken Griffey, Jr., even played together in the outfield for the Seattle Mariners.

In 1987 Cal (left) was joined by his brother Bill, who played alongside him at second base.

As though two Ripkens on a team weren't enough, Bill Ripken joined Cal Jr. in the Orioles' lineup on July 11, 1987. The two played side-by-side in the Baltimore infield—Cal at shortstop and Bill at second base.

Three Ripkens, though, weren't enough to pull the team out of the doldrums. Baltimore finished in sixth place, 31 games out of first.

The next year, things got worse. When the Orioles lost their first six games of the 1988 season, Cal Sr. was fired as manager. He did stay with the team, however, going back to his old spot as the third-base coach. Baltimore's slide continued under Ripken's replacement, Frank Robinson, a Hall of Famer who had starred for the Orioles from 1966 to 1971.

The Orioles lost another 15 games—setting a record for the most losses at the start of the season (21)—before they gave Robinson his first victory as the team's manager. Victories were still hard to come by for the Orioles. They won only 54 games all season and again ended the year in the cellar, 23½ games behind the next worst team in the Eastern Division.

Through these hard times, Cal Jr. at least had his family to console him—and not just his Oriole brother and father. A few years earlier, Cal had met Kelly Geer, and they had begun dating. After the 1987 season, Cal and Kelly had gotten married. In 1989 the Ripkens had a daughter—Rachel Marie.

Three generations of Ripkens. Along with Cal Jr. are his parents, wife, and daughter, Rachel.

Even with so many new events in their private lives, the Ripkens came to think of the Baltimore community as an extension of their family. In the summer of 1988, when Cal contracted to play another three years with the Orioles, he remembered what Eddie Murray had done three years earlier after signing a large contract. Murray had used a portion of the money to finance the first Outward Bound program based in an urban setting. (Outward Bound teaches self-reliance and survival skills.)

Cal and Kelly also wanted to share their good fortune with others. "Kelly and I have a need to put something back into the community that has been so good to us," Cal said when he announced that he and his wife would give $250,000 to start an adult literacy program in Baltimore. Known as the Cal Ripken, Jr., Lifelong Learning Center, the program teaches reading and math to adults.

Cal also joined Murray in establishing a program that provides Oriole home-game tickets for disadvantaged residents of the Baltimore area. Cal has also been active in helping other organizations, including the Children's Center at Johns Hopkins Hospital and the Baltimore School for the Performing Arts.

These off-the-field contributions have been recognized. In 1989 Cal was the first recipient of the Bart Giamatti Award. This national award was created by the Baseball Alumni Team (BAT) in honor of the baseball commissioner who died suddenly on September 1, 1989. In presenting the award, BAT chairman Ralph Branca summed up the sentiments of many people in Baltimore: "Just as Bart Giamatti was a caring person, so is Cal Ripken, Jr."

5

Bouncing Back

Cal signed a multiyear contract with the Orioles and was becoming more involved in community affairs, but 1988 was a difficult year for him on the field. The Orioles had their worst season ever. On top of that, Cal's teammate and close friend Eddie Murray was traded to the Los Angeles Dodgers after the season ended.

The parting between Murray and the Orioles was not a happy one. Murray felt he had been treated poorly by the Orioles, and his final days with the team were agonizing for him. "I can't tell you what it did to me," Murray said. "I couldn't talk to anyone but Cal."

Cal later said of his friend, "I benefited from playing with him and hitting in front of him. I didn't fully realize how much until he left." With Murray gone, would 1989 be even worse than 1988?

No way. Even without Murray's powerful bat behind him in the lineup, Cal came through with another strong season in 1989. He became the first shortstop in history to hit at least 20 homers in eight straight seasons, and he finished third in balloting for the American League's Most Valuable Player (behind Milwaukee's Robin Yount and Ruben Sierra of Texas).

More importantly, the Orioles bounced back as well. They improved their record by more than 30 games and finished second in the American League East, only two games behind the Toronto Blue Jays.

But after this one consistently strong season, both Cal and the Orioles began a roller-coaster ride in 1990. By the end of the season, Baltimore had dropped to fifth place. Cal had an off year, even though he extended his string of 20-homer seasons.

His batting average was only .250, the lowest in any of his nine full seasons in the majors. In the batter's box, he lunged at pitches, getting away from the smooth stroke that had been his trademark for so many years.

The season ended, but Cal kept working on his swing—even at home. Onto the new home Cal and Kelly had bought in Reisterstown, Maryland, Cal had added a gymnasium, complete with a batting cage. Over the winter, he spent many hours practicing in the cage.

"It got to the point where I said, 'Let's go back to the basics, right back to the very beginning, and try to teach yourself how to hit all over again. Act like this is your first year in pro ball.'"

By the time the 1991 season opened, Cal had begun using a new batting stance. Instead of standing upright with his feet close together, he went into a slight crouch with his feet spread apart and his bat held lower.

The new stance worked. In early June, Cal was hitting .344 and leading the league in home runs. He was again a player whom pitchers—and opposing managers—hated to see walk up to the plate.

On June 17th, the Minnesota Twins came to Baltimore riding a 15-game winning streak. They appeared ready to bag number 16 as they nursed a one-run lead with two Orioles out and a runner on second in the last of the ninth. Then Cal came up. Twins manager Tom Kelly deviated from normal strategy by ordering Minnesota's pitcher to walk Ripken intentionally, even though he represented the winning run. Randy Milligan then doubled to left-center to score both runners and end the Twins' streak. Milligan had the big blow, but it was Kelly's fear of Ripken that had set up the winning hit.

Cal throws over Boston's Carlos Quintana to complete a double play in 1991.

Cal's All-Star heroics at SkyDome earned him honors as the game's Most Valuable Player.

In the 1991 All-Star game in Toronto, Cal made his eighth straight All-Star start at shortstop. While he was in Toronto, Cal put on a power show that thrilled SkyDome fans two days in a row. In a home-run hitting contest among the All Stars the day before the game, Cal made it no contest at all. With only 22 swings, he put 12 balls over the wall. One of them bounced off a distant skybox in the fourth deck of the SkyDome.

Despite hitting all those long balls in exhibition, Cal had plenty of power left. In the third inning of the All-Star game, he connected for a long, three-run homer to left-center to give the American League a lead it never relinquished.

For his heroics, Cal was named the game's Most Valuable Player and awarded a new van, which he promptly donated to the Lifelong Learning Center.

A few days later, on July 19, Cal reached a pair of milestones. He hit his 20th home run for the 10th year in a row as he played in his 1,500th consecutive game. The crowd cheered Cal with a long ovation. Now, with his season on track, criticism of the streak was nowhere to be found—a far cry from the boos he had drawn only a year earlier when he passed Everett Scott's consecutive-game mark.

For decades, baseball experts had said that Lou Gehrig's streak of 2,130 straight games would never be challenged.

Cal still had a long way to go. If the streak continued, he wouldn't pass Gehrig until around the All-Star break in 1995. By the time Cal had logged his 1,500th consecutive game, however, the experts were no longer betting against Cal to do it.

Only once was Cal's string of games in danger of being stopped. On the second day of the 1985 season, Cal caught his spikes in second base on a pickoff play. He stayed in the game even though his ankle swelled like a balloon.

Fortunately, the Orioles had only an exhibition game against the Naval Academy the next day, which gave Cal a chance to rest his injured ankle and allowed him to play in Baltimore's next regular-season game.

"I try not to make too much of it myself," Cal said of the streak, "because I have to deal with it on a daily basis. I'm sure that when I sit back someday, it will have a certain meaning. When you're in the middle of it, you don't have time to sit back and reflect."

Through all the ups and downs the Orioles have experienced in the 1980s and 1990s, the one constant has been Ripken's presence at shortstop. While he's done it quietly—never with the flashiness displayed by some—Cal has approached each game with the same competitive spirit he has always felt.

"He's boring to watch for one game, but he's a joy to watch for a season," said Johnny Oates, who succeeded Frank Robinson as the Orioles' manager in June 1991.

Cal's need to excel is evident even when he isn't playing baseball. "I was that way until I started playing pro ball," said teammate Mike Flanagan. "But pro ball is so demanding, I lost some of my desire in other sports. It didn't matter anymore if I won in Ping-Pong. But it matters to him."

Another Oriole, Brady Anderson, said, "In spring training, we have the 12-minute run. You don't have to try. He [Cal] tries. He comes to me before the race and plans it out, how we're going to run it."

But Cal's competitiveness in all types of recreation translates into dedication on the diamond. "He hasn't missed an infield or batting practice in 10 years," said Oates.

With the Orioles again floundering in 1991, the focus was on Cal's individual achievements. As he rolled along, fans and the press wondered if Cal could capture the one award that had so far eluded him—a Gold Glove honoring him as the best-fielding short-stop in the league.

His glovework had been recognized by many people, including George Will, author of a 1990 best-selling book about baseball, *Men at Work*. In the book, Will profiled different baseball notables as models of excellence in managing, pitching, hitting, and defense. To represent the finest in fielding, Will chose Cal.

In 1990 Cal made only three errors all season and had a streak of 95 games in a row with none. But the

Gold Glove went instead to Chicago's Ozzie Guillen, and that sparked some criticism of the selection process.

Former Baltimore star Brooks Robinson, often regarded as the best-fielding third baseman ever, said, "I don't want to detract from Guillen because he's an excellent shortstop. But I would like to have it explained how Cal could play every game, make only three errors and be overlooked. His ability to 'play off' the pitcher is uncanny. He is thinking on every pitch, depending on the tendencies of a batter to hit a certain delivery.

"I was fortunate enough to win 16 Gold Gloves, but you know, they don't seem to mean as much to me because of the way he was passed over."

In 1991 Baltimore finished in sixth place, but Cal reached personal highs in several offensive categories, including batting average (.323), home runs (34), and runs batted in (114).

Again, he was voted major league Player of the Year by the *Sporting News*. Would he be able to add another Most Valuable Player award to his collection?

Playing on a sixth-place team was a disadvantage. The writers who vote for the award sometimes question how valuable a player is if his team hasn't done well. No American Leaguer had ever before received MVP honors while playing on a team with a losing record. Cal became the first.

On November 19, 1991, the votes were revealed. Cal had narrowly outpolled Detroit's Cecil Fielder for the award. One week later came another honor—a Gold Glove for his outstanding play at shortstop.

It was a regal season for Cal, one in which he even met Queen Elizabeth II of England when she accompanied United States President George Bush to a game at Memorial Stadium.

Cal remains busy even after the baseball season is over. His Oriole teammates often come over to his home to work out in his gym. They take batting practice and then choose up sides to play basketball or floor hockey.

Cal's drive to win never quits. In November 1991, in exchange for Kirby Puckett's appearance at a benefit for the Ripken Learning Center, Cal entered Puckett's billiards tournament in Minnesota; Cal won.

Cal also makes public appearances on behalf of the Orioles. But when the business of baseball—whether it be staying in shape or promoting the team—is finished, Cal relaxes at home and spends time with Kelly and Rachel.

Cal is so recognizable all over the United States that it is difficult for him to go out in public without being approached by fans. Cal is gracious and will normally stop to sign an autograph or talk baseball for a few moments. But Cal values the opportunity to get out of the public spotlight from time to time.

Honus Wagner, baseball's greatest shortstop during the early years, was known as the "Flying Dutchman."

As a shortstop for the Chicago Cubs, Ernie Banks was the National League's Most Valuable Player in 1958 and 1959.

60

The family likes to get away for winter vacations, and Cal and Kelly are careful to find a place—often in the Caribbean—where they can be by themselves.

Who are the greatest shortstops of all time? The usual answers include some great names. Honus Wagner—who played for the Pittsburgh Pirates around the turn of the century—is one. Then there's Ernie Banks, who covered shortstop for the Chicago Cubs in the 1950s and 1960s before shifting to first base. Now a lot of people are also answering, "Ripken."

Cal Ripken, Jr., the Oriole Ironman, has earned his place among the greatest.

CAL RIPKEN'S BASEBALL STATISTICS

Minor Leagues

Year	Team (class)	G	AB	R	H	2B	3B	HR	RBI	BB	BA	SA
1978	Bluefield (A)	63	239	27	63	7	1	0	24	24	.264	.301
1979	Miami (A)	105	393	51	119	28	1	5	54	31	.303	.417
	Charlotte (AA)	17	61	6	11	0	1	3	8	3	.180	.361
1980	Charlotte (AA)	144	522	91	144	28	5	25	78	77	.276	.492
1981	Rochester (AAA)	114	437	74	126	31	4	23	75	66	.288	.535
Minor League Totals		343	1652	333	463	94	12	56	239	201	.280	.453

Minor League Highlight:
International League Rookie of the Year, 1981

Major Leagues

Year	Team	G	AB	R	H	2B	3B	HR	RBI	BB	BA	SA
1981	Baltimore	23	39	1	5	0	0	0	0	1	.128	.128
1982	Baltimore	160	598	90	158	32	5	28	93	46	.264	.475
1983	Baltimore	162	663	121	211	47	2	27	102	58	.318	.517
1984	Baltimore	162	641	103	195	37	7	27	86	71	.304	.510
1985	Baltimore	161	642	116	181	32	5	26	110	67	.282	.469
1986	Baltimore	162	627	98	177	35	1	25	81	70	.282	.461
1987	Baltimore	162	624	97	157	28	3	27	98	81	.252	.436
1988	Baltimore	161	575	87	152	25	1	23	81	102	.264	.431
1989	Baltimore	162	646	80	166	30	0	21	93	57	.257	.401
1990	Baltimore	161	600	78	150	28	4	21	84	82	.250	.415
1991	Baltimore	162	650	99	210	46	5	34	114	53	.323	.566
Major League Totals		1638	6305	970	1762	340	33	259	942	688	.279	.458

American League Championship Series

Year	Opponent	G	AB	R	H	2B	3B	HR	RBI	BB	BA	SA
1983	Chicago	4	15	5	6	2	0	0	1	2	.400	.533

World Series

Year	Opponent	G	AB	R	H	2B	3B	HR	RBI	BB	BA	SA
1983	Philadelphia	5	18	2	3	0	0	0	1	3	.167	.167

Major League Highlights:
American League Most Valuable Player, 1983, 1991
The Sporting News Major League Player of the Year, 1983, 1991
American League Gold Glove Award, shortstop, 1991
American League Rookie of the Year, 1982
American League All-Star Team, 1982, 1983, 1984, 1985, 1986, 1987, 1988, 1989, 1990, 1991
All-Star Game Most Valuable Player, 1991
Bart Giamatti Caring Award, 1989

Key
G—games played
AB—at bats
R—runs scored
H—hits

2B—doubles
3B—triples
HR—home runs
RBI—runs batted in

BB—bases on balls
BA—batting average
SA—slugging average

ABOUT THE AUTHOR

Sports historian Stew Thornley is the author of three books, including the best-selling *Holy Cow! The Life and Times of Halsey Hall.*

A former sportscaster at radio stations in Missouri and central Minnesota, Thornley now resides in Minneapolis.